MySQL Stored Routines

Creating Your Own Procedure and Function

A Beginner's Tutorial

Djoni Darmawikarta

Introduction
About This Book
Chapter 1: Stored Procedure Basics
Creating Stored Procedure
Creating Stored Procedure in MySQL Workbench
Hello World
Name of Procedure
Displaying Numeric
Renaming Output Column
Multiple Items in a SELECT
Comment
Updating Procedure
Deleting Procedure
Declaring Variable
Displaying Variable
Data Type
Variable Must be Declared
Same Data Types in One DECLARE
Setting Variable Value
Interacting with Database
Runtime Error Handling
Parameter
Calling within Procedure
Chapter 2: Controlling Program Flow
Control Statements
IF
IF THEN ELSE
IF THEN ELSIF
CASE
CASE_NOT_FOUND Exception
Searched CASE
LOOP
Basic LOOP
Nested LOOP
WHILE loop
Chapter 3: Processing Query Rows
SELECT INTO

One Row Only
SELECT for UPDATE
CURSOR

Chapter 4: Creating Stored Function
Using Stored Function
Creating Stored Function in MySQL Workbench

Appendix A: Installing MySQL Server and Workbench
Downloading MySQL Community Edition
Installing MySQL Community Edition
Installing MySQL Workbench

Introduction

Welcome to *MySQL Stored Routines: Creating Your Own (User-Defined) Procedure and Function, A Beginner's Tutorial.* This book is for you if you want to learn MySQL's stored routines the easy way. By particularly following the book examples you will quickly gain practical skills.

MySQL stored routines are programs you write and compile. They are then stored in the database. Other programs, and other users, who have the permission, can then use your routines.

A routine can be a procedure or function. It can have both SQL and procedural statements. The SQL statements are used to access *sets* of data stored in the database, while the procedural statements are used to process *individual* data item, and to control the program flow using the if-then-else and looping structures.

About This Book

This book consists of four chapters and two appendixes. This section gives you an overview of each chapter and appendixes.

Chapter 1, "Stored Procedure Basics", walks you through the fundamental structure and features of stored procedure.

Chapter 2, "Controlling Program Flow", covers the procedural constructs, including if, if-then, loop, and case.

Chapter 3, "Processing Query Rows", shows you especially how to use cursor to handle multiple rows returned by a query.

Chapter 4, "Creating Stored Function", introduces stored function; you will learn how to create and use stored function in this chapter.

Appendix A, "Installing MySQL", is your step-by-step guide to install MySQL Community Edition.

Chapter 1: Stored Procedure Basics

Stored procedure is a database object. You write a stored procedure as a CREATE PROCEDURE statement; then compile it by executing the statement. When the compilation is successful the procedure object is stored in the database where you compile it. The procedure is then available to other programs and other users who have the permission to use it.

Creating Stored Procedure

The CREATE PROCEDURE, which is a SQL statement, has the following syntax.

```
CREATE PROCEDURE procedure_name(parameters)
BEGIN
DECLARE declaration_statement;
. . .
executable_statement;
. . .
END;
```

The procedure contains declaration and executable statements within the BEGIN ... END block.

The parameter is optional. Technically you can create a procedure that does not have any declaration and executable statement, but you never create real-world procedure that does not do anything.

Every declaration statement and executable statement must be terminated by a semicolon (;)

Creating Stored Procedure in MySQL Workbench

To create a new procedure, right-click the Stored Procedures under your target schema (database), such as our *mybook* schema; and then, select the Create Stored Procedure.

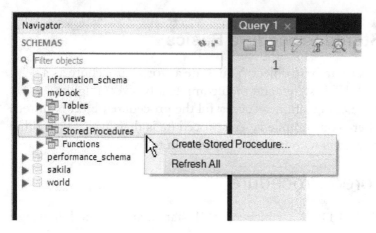

You will get a skeleton procedure.

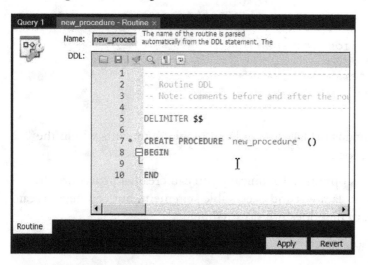

Change the name of the procedure to the name you want; for example, *about_nothing*, then click the Apply button. You will see a pop-up window that looks like the following.

The backticks (`) enclosing the procedure name are optional. From now on I will not have these backticks in this book.

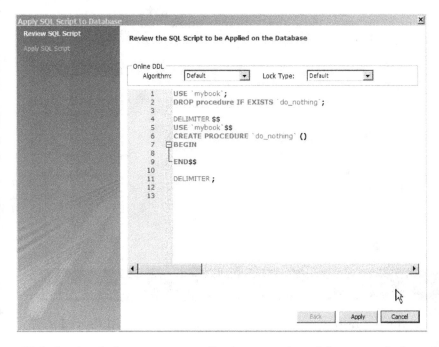

Click the Apply button to compile the procedure. The next window shows the compilation is successful and the procedure object is available in the database.

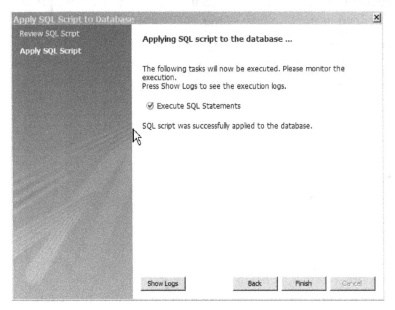

Click the Finish button to close the pop-up window, and you are back to the source editor window.

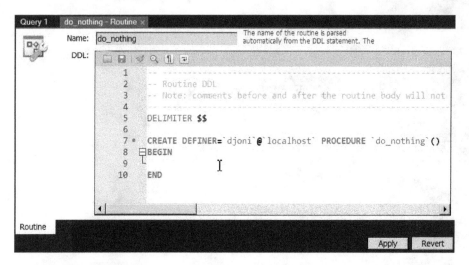

You will see the do_nothing procedure listed under the Stored Procedures folder.

The DEFINER clause is optional. It specifies the user whose privileges will be applied when the procedure is used (called). In the above example that user is djoni as defined in the localhost server.

To test the procedure, on the Query tab call the procedure, execute a call statement to the procedure, like the following. Our do_nothing procedure execution gets completed successfully as indicated by the green tick on the Output panel.

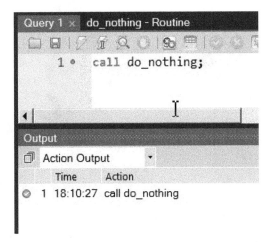

Hello World

Without further ado, let's create our first stored procedure that does something, showing nothing else than the familiar Hello World! greeting.

Insert just one statement in between the BEGIN and END, a select 'Hello World!'. This select statement displays its parameter, which in our case is the Hello World! literal string. Note that a string literal must be enclosed by single quotes, like the **'Hello World!'**.

Note that if you do not want to type in the source code yourself, you can copy it from here and paste into your workbench.

```
CREATE PROCEDURE hello_world()
BEGIN
select 'Hello World!';
ENDEND
```

When you call the hello_world procedure after successfully compiling it, you will get the expected output, the Hello World!, on the Result Grid like the following.

Name of Procedure

You must observe the following rules when naming a procedure.

- The name of a procedure can contain only letters (a-z, A-Z), digits 0-9, dollar sign ($), and underscore (_);
- Has a maximum length of 64 characters procedure_name;
- Must be unique within the database
- Is case insensitive

When you try an invalid name, for example, 007+Bond, you will see a red cross mark on the line number.

```
1    -- ---------------------------
2    -- Routine DDL
3    -- Note: comments before and afte
4    -- ---------------------------
5    DELIMITER $$
6
7    CREATE PROCEDURE 007+Bond ()
8    BEGIN
9
10   END
```

As we already have a hello_world procedure, you cannot create a Hello_World procedure within the same database. When you try to compile, you will get an error message.

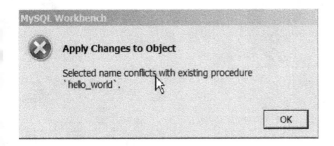

Displaying Numeric

The SELECT can also display numeric data. The following procedure will display the result of the result of the addition, **10**.

```
CREATE PROCEDURE display_numeric ()
BEGIN
select 1 + 9;
END
```

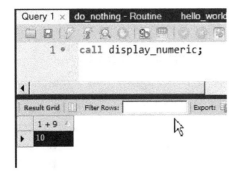

In this book, we use the SELECT, as we want to see immediate output, to check if our procedure is good. In real-world procedures you can use SELECT statements during development for testing and debugging.

Renaming Output Column

You might have noticed the column heading of the output is the parameter of the select statement, for example the 1 + 9. You can rename the heading using the AS clause.

```
CREATE PROCEDURE rename_heading ()
BEGIN
```

```
select 1 + 9 as GREETING;
END
```

The output will now be as follows.

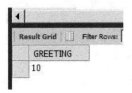

Multiple Items in a SELECT

You can have more than one item in one SELECT using the CONCAT MySQL built-in function.

In the following **multiple_items** procedure, three items are combined (concatenated): "**Hello World!**", "**...**" and **1 + 9** (which equals to **10**)

```
CREATE PROCEDURE multiple_items ()
BEGIN
select concat('Hello World!',' ... ', 1 + 9) AS
3_items_combined;
END
```

The output is:

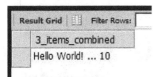

Comment

A short break here before we explore more functional features.

Comment lines within the source program of a stored procedure can be useful as inline documentation. Comments are ignored, they are not executable.

Comment comes in two flavors: Single and multi-line. Any text in a source code following a double dash -- until the end of the line, is a single-line comment.

When a /* mark is encountered, all texts and lines a closing */ mark is encountered, is a multi-line comment.

Here is the previous multiple_items procedure, renamed as **comments**, with comments added. The **comments** procedure produces the same output as the multiple_items procedure; the comments do not affect the function of the procedure.

```
CREATE PROCEDURE comments()
BEGIN
/* To display three items combined
into one */
-- Use the concat built-in function
select concat('Hello World!',' ... ', 1 + 9) AS
3_items_combined; -- rename the heading
END
```

The output is the same as that of the multiple_items procedure.

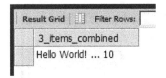

Result Grid	Filter Rows:
3_items_combined
Hello World! ... 10

Updating Procedure

You can update an existing procedure by right-clicking the procedure.

When you finish editing the procedure, click the Apply button.

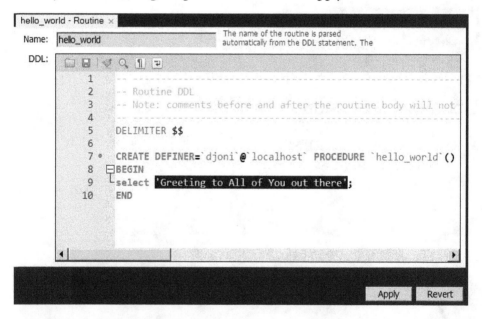

Deleting Procedure

To delete a procedure, right-click the procedure and select Drop Stored Procedure; the procedure will no longer be in the list.

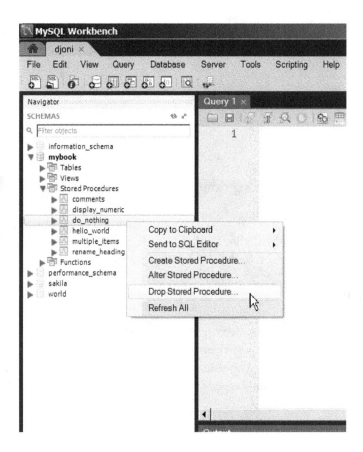

Declaring Variable

The statement syntax to declare a variable is:

```
DECLARE variable_name datatype DEFAULT value;
```

The datatype is mandatory; DEFAULT is optional.

You must observe the following when naming a variable:
- The name of a procedure can contain only letters (a-z, A-Z), digits 0-9, dollar sign ($), and underscore (_);
- Must be unique within the database
- Is case insensitive

When you try an invalid name, you will see a red cross mark; the @ character is the culprit in the following example.

```
 5    DELIMITER $$
 6
 7 •  CREATE PROCEDURE `invalid_variable_name` ()
 8    ┌BEGIN
 9 ▣  │ DECLARE bad@var CHAR(10);
10    └END
```

Note that:
- you will unlikely need to give a long name to a variable, MySQL allows longer than 255 characters.
- when you don't assign a default value to a variable during its declaration, its value will be NULL until you change it.
- a declaration statement must be terminated with a semicolon.

Displaying Variable

The parameter of a SELECT statement does not need to be a *literal*. In the following display_variable procedure the parameter is the greeting variable. The string literal stored in the greeting variable, Hello World!, will be displayed. The Hello World! Value gets stored in the greeting variable during its declaration thanks to the **default** clause.

```
CREATE PROCEDURE display_variable ()
BEGIN
declare greeting char(12) default 'Hello World!';
select greeting;
END
```

The value of the variable is:

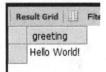

Result Grid	Filte
greeting
Hello World!

Data Type

When you declare a variable you must specify its type. You have seen the use of CHAR data type, which is used to store fixed length string of characters.

Other commonly used data types are:

- VARCHAR (m) - to store a variable length string of characters to a maximum of m characters.
- INTEGER - to store numeric integer type of data
- DECIMAL (p, s) - to store numeric data with precision of p digits and scale of s digits
- DATE – to store date
- TIMESTAMP– to store date and time

The following data_types procedure show the use of the above first four data types.

```
CREATE PROCEDURE data_types ()
BEGIN
DECLARE v VARCHAR(5) DEFAULT 'MySQL';
DECLARE i INTEGER(2) DEFAULT 11;
DECLARE d DECIMAL(4,2) DEFAULT 23.45;
DECLARE dt DATE DEFAULT '2014-09-20';
select v;
select i;
select d;
select dt;
END
```

The output is on four different tabs for each of the four selects: Result 1, 2, 3 and 4.

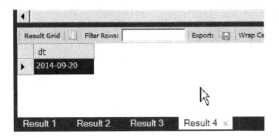

Here is an example of the use of TIMESTAMP variable. localtimestamp is a built-in function that returns your local date and time at the time you call the procedure.

```
CREATE PROCEDURE local_ts ()
BEGIN
declare ts datetime default localtimestamp;
END
```

Here is the output when I called the local_ts.

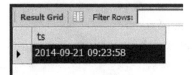

Variable Must be Declared

You must declare a variable before you can use it in an executable statement.

In the following no_declaration procedure, the greeting variable is not declared.

```
CREATE PROCEDURE no_declaration ()
BEGIN
select greeting;
END
```

Though it is compiled successfully, when you call the procedure, it fails.

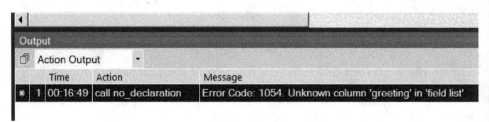

Same Data Types in One DECLARE

You can declare more than one variables in one DECLARE statement as long as they all have the same data type.

```
CREATE PROCEDURE same_datatype ()
BEGIN
DECLARE date_one, date_two DATE DEFAULT '2014-09-13';
SELECT date_one;
SELECT date_two;
END
```

The same default value are on the two output tabs.

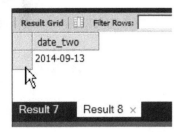

Setting Variable Value

You use the SET statement with equal operator (=) to set a variable value. The SET statement has the following syntax.

```
SET variable = value;
```

The *value* can be a literal (data value), variable or expression.

In the following set_var procedure the value 'MySQL' of variable w is changed to 'Welcome to MySQL' by the SET statement. In this SET statement the *value* is an expression CONCAT('Welcome to ', w).

```
CREATE PROCEDURE set_var ()
BEGIN
DECLARE w VARCHAR(25) DEFAULT 'MySQL';
SET w = CONCAT('Welcome to ', w);
SELECT CONCAT(w);
END
```

Here is the output.

You also use a SET statement to store the result of numeric computation. The * is a multiplication operator; the ^, exponentiation.

```
CREATE PROCEDURE computation ()
BEGIN
DECLARE x, y, z DECIMAL(4,2) DEFAULT 1.1;
SET y = (x - 0.1) * 5 + (z + 0.9) ^ 2 ;
SELECT y;
```

END

The output is:

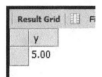

Interacting with Database

To interact with the database, you use SQL statements in the procedure.

Note that this book does not specifically cover SQL. To quickly gain SQL skill, read my book, *"SQL for MySQL"*

The following sql_statements procedure has an INSERT, UPDATE and DELETE SQL statements. The statements change the rows of the product table.

```
CREATE PROCEDURE sql_statements ()
BEGIN
INSERT INTO product VALUES (9999, 'Test', NULL, NULL, NULL);
UPDATE product SET price = 0 WHERE p_code = 9999;
DELETE FROM product WHERE p_code = 9;
END$$
```

To try the example, you need to create the product table by executing the following SQL statement.

```
Query 1 ×
 1 • ⊟CREATE TABLE product (
 2        p_code INTEGER NOT NULL,
 3        p_name VARCHAR(15),
 4        p_type VARCHAR(6),
 5        price DECIMAL(4 , 2 ),
 6        launch_dt DATE,
 7        PRIMARY KEY (p_code)
 8     └)
 9     ;
10
```

Then, insert the six rows into the table by executing the following SQL statement.

```
Query 1 ×
1 •   INSERT INTO product
2         VALUES (1, 'Apple', 'Fruit', 1, '2014-5-1'),
3         (2, 'Broccoli', 'Veggie', 2, '2014-5-2'),
4         (3, 'Carrot', 'Veggie', 3, '2014-5-3'),
5         (4, 'Mango', 'Fruit', 4, '2014-5-4'),
6         (5, 'Grape', I'Fruit', 5, '2014-5-5'),
7         (9, 'Kale', 'Veggie', NULL, '2014-9-13')
8     ;
9
```

Here are the rows before you call the procedure.

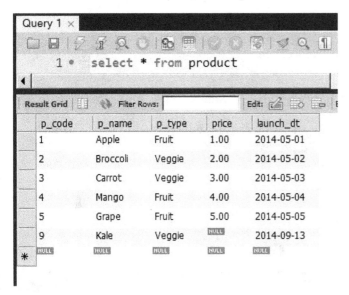

After calling the procedure, the rows will be as follows. (To see the rows execute a SELECT * FROM product statement)

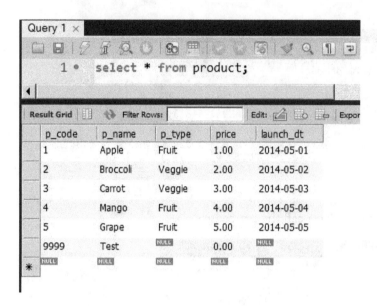

Runtime Error Handling

When you call the following runtime_err procedure, it fails. The SELECT statement is not executed, the procedure is aborted.

```
CREATE PROCEDURE runtime_err ()
BEGIN
INSERT INTO product VALUES
(1, 'Apple', NULL, NULL, NULL);
SELECT 'After the INSERT statment';
END
```

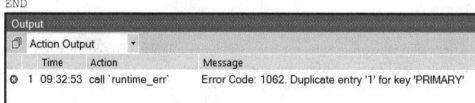

We can handle this runtime error by declaring a handler demonstrated in the following *1602_handler* procedure.

As the error number as seen in the error message is 1062, we add a **DECLARE CONTINUE HANDLER FOR 1062** to trap the 1062 error caused by the failure of the INSERT statement. The CONTINUE option in the declaration signals the handler that we want the procedure to continue if the INSERT statement fails, to execute the SELECT handler_msg statement.

```
CREATE PROCEDURE 1062_handler ()
BEGIN
DECLARE handler_msg VARCHAR(30);
DECLARE CONTINUE HANDLER FOR 1062
SET handler_msg = 'After the INSERT statement';
INSERT INTO product VALUES
(1, 'Apple', NULL, NULL, NULL);
SELECT handler_msg;
END
```

When you call the procedure, it successfully gets completed, the value of the handler_msg is displayed.

You can ask the handler to exit the procedure by changing the CONTINUE option to EXIT as shown in the following 1062_handler_exit procedure.

```
CREATE PROCEDURE 1062_handler_exit()
 BEGIN
DECLARE handler_msg VARCHAR(30);
 DECLARE EXIT HANDLER FOR 1062 SET handler_msg = 'After the
      INSERT statement';
 INSERT INTO product VALUES
    (1, 'Apple', NULL, NULL, NULL);
SELECT handler_msg;
END
```

When you call the procedure and the INSERT fails, the procedure is exited; the SELECT handler_msg is skipped, it is not executed. When you run the procedure, it will get successfully completed, but the handler_msg is not displayed.

Parameter

Recall the syntax of the CREATE PROCEDURE statement:

```
CREATE PROCEDURE procedure_name(parameters)
```

```
BEGIN
DECLARE declaration_statement;
. . .
executable_statement;
. . .
END;
```

You can pass data when you call a procedure that has parameters defined for the data. The following increase_price procedure has two parameters, the first is the code of the product you want to increase the price and the increase in percentage.

```
CREATE PROCEDURE increase_price(code varchar(2), increase
      decimal(2,0))
BEGIN
update product set price = price + (price * increase/100)
      where p_code = code;
commit;
END
```

Note that you must define the datatype of the parameter.

When you call the procedure you must supply the values for the parameters.

```
call increase_price(1,10);
```

Assuming the rows of the product table are as follows

p_code	p_name	p_type	price	launch_dt
1	Apple	Fruit	1.00	2014-05-01
2	Broccoli	Veggie	2.00	2014-05-02
3	Carrot	Veggie	4.00	2014-05-03
4	Mango	Fruit	5.00	2014-05-04
5	Grape	Fruit	6.00	2014-05-05
NULL	NULL	NULL	NULL	NULL

After the call to the increase_procedure, the Apple's price will increase to 1.10

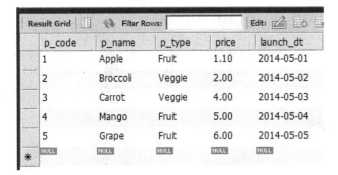

Calling within Procedure

You can call a procedure within another procedure. The following main procedure has three of the procedures we already created earlier.

```
CREATE PROCEDURE main()
BEGIN
call do_nothing;
call hello_world;
call rename_heading;
END
```

When you then call main, two outputs will be displayed, the do_nothing does not produce anything.

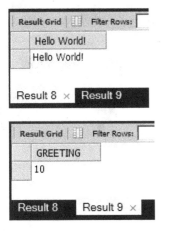

Chapter 2: Controlling Program Flow

The executable statements in all preceding examples are executed linearly from top to the bottom of the programs. In this chapter you will learn conditional and loop statements to control the execution flow of a program.

Control Statements

To control program flows, you use conditional and loop statements.

IF

The IF control statements have three versions: IF THEN, IF THEN ELSE, and IF THEN ELSEIF.

IF THEN

The syntax of the IF THEN statement is.

```
IF condition THEN
   statements;
END IF;
```

Only if the condition is true the statements will be executed.

In the following procedure, the INSERT statement will only be executed when the launch_dt of Apple is earlier than April 5, 2014.

The SELECT … INTO statement is a SELECT query. It returns a row from the table.

```
CREATE PROCEDURE if_then ()
BEGIN
DECLARE launch_dt_var DATE;
   SELECT launch_dt INTO launch_dt_var
   FROM product WHERE p_name = 'Apple';
      IF launch_dt_var < '20140705' THEN
         INSERT INTO product VALUES
         (44, 'Newer Apple', 'Fruit', 1.5, CURRENT_DATE);
      END IF;
END
```

After you create the if_then procedure and you call it, the Newer Apple will be inserted as the Apple's launch_dt is 2014-05-01.

Result Grid	Filter Rows:			Edit:	
p_code	p_name	p_type	price	launch_dt	
1	Apple	Fruit	1.00	2014-05-01	
2	Broccoli	Veggie	2.00	2014-05-02	
3	Carrot	Veggie	3.00	2014-05-03	
4	Mango	Fruit	4.00	2014-05-04	
5	Grape	Fruit	5.00	2014-05-05	
44	Newer Ap...	Fruit	1.50	2014-09-21	
9999	Test	NULL	0.00	NULL	
*	NULL	NULL	NULL	NULL	NULL

IF THEN ELSE

The syntax of the IF THEN ELSE statement is.

```
IF condition THEN
   if_statements;
ELSE
   else_statements;
END IF;
```

An IF THEN ELSE executes its if_statements if the condition is true. If the condition is false, the else_statements are executed.

The following if_then_else procedure has an IF THEN ELSE statement. The SELECT statement on the ELSE clause will display its string unless the launch_dt of Apple is earlier than April 5, 2014.

```
CREATE PROCEDURE if_then_else ()
BEGIN
DECLARE launch_dt_var DATE;
SELECT launch_dt INTO launch_dt_var
FROM product WHERE p_name = 'Apple';
IF launch_dt_var > '20140705' THEN
INSERT INTO product VALUES
(55, 'Newest Apple', 'Fruit', 1.5, CURRENT_DATE);
ELSE SELECT ('No newer apple');
END IF;
END
```

As the Apple's launch_dt is 2014-05-01, the "No newer apple" string is displayed.

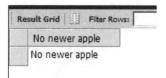

IF THEN ELSIF

If you need multiple ELSE's, then use an IF THEN ELSIF statement. Its syntax is as follows.

```
IF condition_1 THEN
  statements_1;
ELSEIF condition_2 THEN
  statements_2;
ELSEIF ...
[ ELSE
  else_statements ]
END IF;
```

The IF THEN ELSEIF statement executes only the first statement for which its condition is true; the remaining conditions are not evaluated. If no condition is true, then the else_statements are executed, if they exist. The ELSE is optional.

The following if_then_elseif procedure has an IF THEN ELSEIF statement. As the Apple's launch_dt is 2014-05-01 and its price is 1, the "No newer apple" is displayed.

```
CREATE PROCEDURE if_then_elseif()
BEGIN
DECLARE price_var DECIMAL(4,2);
DECLARE launch_dt_var DATE;
SELECT launch_dt, price INTO launch_dt_var, price_var
FROM product WHERE p_name = 'Apple';
IF launch_dt_var > '20140705' THEN
INSERT INTO product VALUES
(66, 'Better Apple', 'Fruit', 1.5, CURRENT_DATE);
ELSEIF price_var <= 0.9 THEN
SELECT 'Please increase the price';
```

```
ELSE
SELECT ('No newer apple');
END IF;
END
```

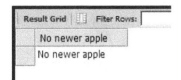

CASE

If you have many decision alternatives, a CASE statement might be a better a conditional statement than the IF ELSIF statement. You can choose one of the two CASE statements: Simple or Searched.

Simple CASE

The syntax of the Simple CASE statement is as follows.

```
CASE selector
WHEN selector_value_1 THEN then_statements_1;
WHEN selector_value_2 THEN then_statements_2;
WHEN ...
[ELSE else_statements]
END CASE;
```

The selector is a literal or a variable.

The simple CASE statement runs its first then_statements for which their selector_value equals the selector; the remaining WHEN statements are not executed. If no selector_value equals the selector, the CASE statement runs the else_statements.

In the Simple CASE statement of the following simple_case procedure, the selector is the price variable. The CASE statement has three WHEN's; the output displayed depends on the price of the Apple. If the price not 1 or 2 or 3, then the displayed output is "No match".

```
CREATE PROCEDURE simple_case()
BEGIN
DECLARE price_var DECIMAL(4,2);
SELECT price INTO price_var
```

```
       FROM product WHERE p_name = 'Apple';
   CASE price_var
     WHEN 1 THEN SELECT('Price is $1');
     WHEN 2 THEN SELECT('Price is $2');
     WHEN 3 THEN SELECT('Expensive');
       ELSE SELECT('No match');
   END CASE;
END
```

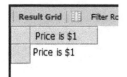

CASE_NOT_FOUND Exception

If there is no match and ELSE is not available you will get an error message as demonstrated in the following case_not_found procedure.

```
CREATE PROCEDURE case_not_found()
BEGIN
DECLARE price_var DECIMAL(4,2);
   SELECT price INTO price_var
       FROM product WHERE p_name = 'Apple';
   CASE price_var
   WHEN 1.5 THEN
     SELECT('Price is $1');
   WHEN 2 THEN
     SELECT('Price is $2');
   WHEN 3 THEN
     SELECT('Expensive');
   END CASE;
END
```

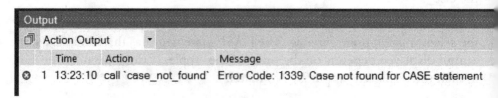

You can add an exception handler to mitigate the issue as demonstrated in the following case_not_found procedure. Note that the error code is 1339.

```
CREATE PROCEDURE case_not_found_handler()
```

```
BEGIN
DECLARE price_var DECIMAL(4,2);
DECLARE handler_msg VARCHAR(30);
DECLARE CONTINUE HANDLER FOR 1339
 SET handler_msg = 'Our cases are not complete';
   SELECT price INTO price_var
   FROM product WHERE p_name = 'Apple';
  CASE price_var
  WHEN 1.5 THEN
    SELECT('Price is $1');
   WHEN 2 THEN
    SELECT('Price is $2');
  WHEN 3 THEN
    SELECT('Expensive');
  END CASE;
 SELECT handler_msg;
END
```

Here is the output when you call the procedure.

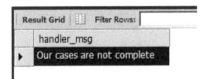

Searched CASE

A Searched CASE statement has the following syntax. Notice that it does not have a selector.

```
CASE
WHEN condition_1 THEN statements_1
WHEN condition_2 THEN statements_2
WHEN...
ELSE else_statements
END CASE;
```

While in the Simple CASE, the "condition" of selecting which statements to execute is the comparison of the selection_value to the selector for equality, in Searched CASE the condition is within each WHEN.

The searched CASE statement executes the first statement for which its condition is true. Remaining conditions are not evaluated. If no condition is true, the CASE statement runs else_statements if they exist and raises the predefined exception CASE_NOT_FOUND otherwise.

The conditions are independent; they do not need to have any kind of relationship.

Two or more conditions can be true, but only the first in the order you have in the source program (top to bottom) will be granted and its statements executed.

The following searched_case procedure a Searched CASE with two conditions.

```
CREATE PROCEDURE searched_case()
BEGIN
DECLARE
  max_price, avg_price DECIMAL(6,2);
 SELECT MAX(price) INTO max_price FROM product;
SELECT AVG(price) INTO avg_price FROM product;
 CASE
    -- reduce price
  WHEN max_price > 5 THEN
     UPDATE product SET price = price - (price * .01);
    -- increase price
  WHEN avg_price < 3.5 THEN
     UPDATE product SET price = price + (price * .01);
END CASE;
END
```

Assuming our product table has the following rows.

p_code	p_name	p_type	price	launch_dt
1	Apple	Fruit	1.00	2014-05-01
2	Broccoli	Veggie	2.00	2014-05-02
3	Carrot	Veggie	3.00	2014-05-03
4	Mango	Fruit	4.00	2014-05-04
5	Grape	Fruit	5.00	2014-05-05
NULL	NULL	NULL	NULL	NULL

when you call the searched_case procedure, the first condition is not satisfied, and then, the second condition is satisfied. Hence the rows of the product table are now as follows.

p_code	p_name	p_type	price	launch_dt
1	Apple	Fruit	1.01	2014-05-01
2	Broccoli	Veggie	2.02	2014-05-02
3	Carrot	Veggie	3.03	2014-05-03
4	Mango	Fruit	4.04	2014-05-04
5	Grape	Fruit	5.05	2014-05-05
* NULL	NULL	NULL	NULL	NULL

(Result Grid — Filter Rows: — Edit:)

LOOP

Loops allow you to repeat the same statements. LOOP statement comes in three flavours: Basic, Nested, and Fixed Iteration.

Basic LOOP

The structure of the Basic LOOP is

```
Label: LOOP
statements
END LOOP label;
```

The statements run from the first to the last before the END LOOP, and then back to the first, until an EXIT conditional statement, which should be provided within the loop, is satisfied on which the loop is terminated.

The label is optional, but it helps clarifies the scope of the loop.

The loop in the following basic_loop procedure iterates three times. On the fourth iteration num = 4, hence the exit condition is satisfied, the next statement after the loop is executed, and then the program ends.

```
CREATE PROCEDURE basic_loop()
DECLARE num INTEGER DEFAULT 1;
basic_loop: LOOP
    IF num > 3 THEN -- loop three times only
        LEAVE basic_loop;
```

```
    END IF;
      SELECT CONCAT('In loop: num = ', num);
      SET num = num + 1;
END LOOP basic_loop;
  -- On EXIT, execute the following statement
  SELECT CONCAT('After loop: num = ', num);
END
```

When you call the procedure you will get the following outputs on four tabs.

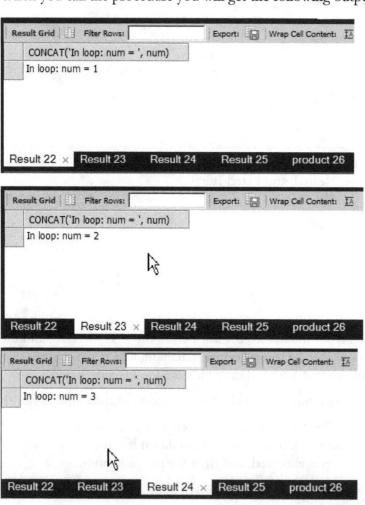

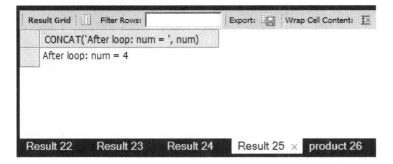

Nested LOOP

You can nest a loop. In the following nested_loop procedure, the inner loop is nested within the outer loop. For every iteration of the outer loop, the inner loop is iterated twice.

```
CREATE PROCEDURE nested_loop()
BEGIN
DECLARE counter1, counter2 INTEGER DEFAULT 1;
 parent: LOOP
    IF counter1 > 2 THEN LEAVE parent; -- loop twice
    END IF;
      SELECT CONCAT('Outer loop: counter1 = ',counter1);
        SET counter1 = counter1 + 1;
        child: LOOP
           IF counter2 > 2 THEN LEAVE child; -- loop twice
              END IF;
    SELECT CONCAT ('Inner loop: counter2 = ', counter2);
   SET counter2 = counter2 + 1;
   END LOOP;
  SET counter2 = 1;
 END LOOP;
  SELECT CONCAT('After loop: counter1 = ', counter1);
END
```

Here are the seven outputs when you call the procedure.

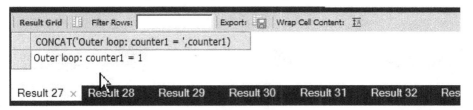

Result Grid | Filter Rows: | Export: | Wrap Cell Content: ‡A

CONCAT ('Inner loop: counter2 = ', counter2)

Inner loop: counter2 = 1

Result 27 | Result 28 × | Result 29 | Result 30 | Result 31 | Result 32 | Res

---

Result Grid | Filter Rows: | Export: | Wrap Cell Content: ‡A

CONCAT ('Inner loop: counter2 = ', counter2)

Inner loop: counter2 = 2

Result 27 | Result 28 | Result 29 × | Result 30 | Result 31 | Result 32 | Res

---

Result Grid | Filter Rows: | Export: | Wrap Cell Content: ‡A

CONCAT('Outer loop: counter1 = ',counter1)

Outer loop: counter1 = 2

Result 27 | Result 28 | Result 29 | Result 30 × | Result 31 | Result 32 | Res

---

Result Grid | Filter Rows: | Export: | Wrap Cell Content: ‡A

CONCAT ('Inner loop: counter2 = ', counter2)

Inner loop: counter2 = 1

Result 27 | Result 2? | Result 29 | Result 30 | Result 31 × | Result 32 | Res

---

Result Grid | Filter Rows: | Export: | Wrap Cell Content: ‡A

CONCAT ('Inner loop: counter2 = ', counter2)

Inner loop: counter2 = 2

Result 27 | Result 28 | Result 29 | Result 30 | Result 31 | Result 32 × | Res

---

Result Grid | Filter Rows: | Export: | Wrap Cell Content: ‡A

CONCAT('After loop: counter1 = ', counter1)

After loop: counter1 = 3

Result 27 | Result 28 | Result 29 | Result 30 | Result 31 | Result 32 | Res

WHILE loop

You can also use a WHILE to form a loop. Its syntax is as follows.

```
WHILE condition
DO statements;
END WHILE;
```

The statements in while will be executed as long as the condition is true. You must ensure the while can terminate.

In the following while_proc procedure, the loop terminates when i = 4. Notice that the i variable used here must be declared; while in the previous nested_loop procedure, it should not. When i reaches 4 the loop ends, the statements inside it are not executed.

```
CREATE PROCEDURE while_proc()
BEGIN
DECLARE i INTEGER DEFAULT 1;
  WHILE i < 4
    DO
      SELECT CONCAT('Iteration number: ',i);
      SET i = i +1;
  END WHILE;
END
```

When you call the procedure, the output will be as follows.

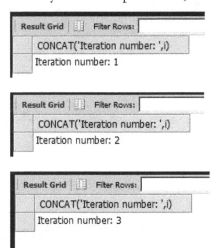

Chapter 3: Processing Query Rows

In chapter 1, you learned to use SQL for maintaining data using the INSERT, UPDATE and DELETE statements. These statements are just the regular SQL statements. In this chapter you will learn SELECT statement, which is not the same as its regular statement.

SELECT INTO

If you need to query only one row, use the SELECT INTO statement that has the following syntax.

The SELECT with INTO syntax is:

```
SELECT select_columns INTO into_columns FROM ...
```

The into_columns must be in the sequence and the same datatype as those of the select_columns.

The following select_into procedure has three INTO columns.

```
CREATE PROCEDURE select_into()
BEGIN
DECLARE name_v VARCHAR(20);
DECLARE price_v DECIMAL(6,2);
  SELECT p_name, price
   INTO name_v, price_v
   FROM product
   WHERE p_code = 1;
   SELECT CONCAT('The price of our ', name_v, ' is $ ',
      price_v) AS price;
END
```

One Row Only

A SELECT INTO must return exactly one row.

The following multiple_rows procedure fails as its query returns more than one row.

```
CREATE PROCEDURE multiple_rows()
BEGIN
DECLARE name_v  VARCHAR(20);
DECLARE price_v DECIMAL(6,2);
 SELECT p_name, price
 INTO name_v, price_v
  FROM product;
END
```

Calling the procedure, you will get an error message.

You can use the exception to handle this error 1172 as in the following multi_rows_handler procedure.

```
CREATE PROCEDURE multi_rows_handler()
 BEGIN
 DECLARE name_v  VARCHAR(20);
 DECLARE price_v DECIMAL(6,2);
 DECLARE handler_msg VARCHAR(30);
 DECLARE CONTINUE HANDLER FOR 1172 SET handler_msg = 'Multi-
     rows handler';
   SELECT p_name, price
   INTO name_v, price_v
   FROM product;
 SELECT handler_msg;
END
```

When you call the procedure, the exception-handler will displays the exception message.

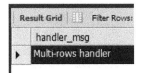

SELECT for UPDATE

When you need to first SELECT and then UPDATE the selected row, and you want to be sure the selected row is not updated by any other SQL statement while you are updating it, you can lock the selected row using the FOR UPDATE clause as shown in the following for_update procedure.

```
CREATE PROCEDURE for_update()
 BEGIN
 DECLARE code_v VARCHAR(20);
   SELECT p_code INTO code_v FROM product
   WHERE p_code = 1 FOR UPDATE;
   UPDATE product SET price = 1 WHERE p_code = 1;
END
```

When you call the procedure, the Apple's price will be updated to 1 even when the row is being accessed by any other user or application.

p_code	p_name	p_type	price	launch_dt
1	Apple	Fruit	1.00	2014-05-01
2	Broccoli	Veggie	2.02	2014-05-02
3	Carrot	Veggie	3.03	2014-05-03
4	Mango	Fruit	4.04	2014-05-04
5	Grape	Fruit	5.05	2014-05-05
NULL	NULL	NULL	NULL	NULL

CURSOR

To handle multiple rows, we need to use CURSOR. A cursor stores the rows return by the cursor's query; the cursor then facilitates you to access the rows **one by one**.

You specify the query that you use to get the rows from a database by declaring a cursor. The declaration syntax is:

```
DECLARE
CURSOR cursor_name IS query;
```

Once you declare a cursor, in the executable part, you go through the cursor's life cycle, i.e. open the cursor; fetch a row, when you are done with the cursor, close it.

The syntax of the OPEN, FETCH, and CLOSE statements are respectively:

```
OPEN cursor;
```

```
FETCH cursor INTO variables;

CLOSE cursor;
```

The FETCH has an INTO clause, which stores the row of the cursor into the variables. All data types of the variables must match with the data types of the columns of the cursor's row.

In the following product_cur procedure we declare a cursor named c. The c cursor stores all product rows returned by its query.

The procedure has only one FETCH, which fetches the first row from the cursor.

```
CREATE PROCEDURE product_cur()
 BEGIN
 DECLARE code_v, name_v VARCHAR(20);
 DECLARE launch_dt_v DATE;
 DECLARE c CURSOR FOR
     SELECT p_code, p_name, launch_dt FROM product;
   OPEN c;
   FETCH c INTO code_v, name_v, launch_dt_v;
   SELECT CONCAT(code_v,' ',name_v,' ', launch_dt_v);
   CLOSE c;
END
```

The output you see is.

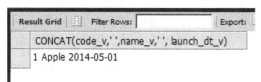

To access more than one row from a cursor, use loop, as demonstrated in the following use_loop procedure. You must prevent infinite loop, hence we use the NOT FOUND handler is used to leave the loop.

Note that the LEAVE refers to the label of the loop.

```
CREATE PROCEDURE loop_cur()
 BEGIN
 DECLARE no_more_row INTEGER DEFAULT FALSE;
 DECLARE code_v, name_v VARCHAR(20);
 DECLARE launch_dt_v DATE;
 DECLARE c CURSOR FOR
```

```
        SELECT p_code, p_name, launch_dt;
DECLARE CONTINUE HANDLER FOR NOT FOUND SET no_more_row =
        TRUE;
OPEN c;
 more_row: LOOP
        FETCH c INTO code_v, name_v, launch_dt_v;
        IF no_more_row THEN LEAVE more_row;
        END IF;
        SELECT CONCAT(code_v,' ',name_v,' ',launch_dt_v);
 END LOOP more_row;
 CLOSE c;
END
```

When you call the procedure, you will get the outputs in as many tabs as the number of rows in the product table.

Chapter 4: Creating Stored Function

A stored function is also a database object. While a stored procedure does something, a stored function returns something.

The SQL statement for creating a stored function is as follows.

```
CREATE FUNCTION function_name(parameters)
RETURNS datatype;
BEGIN
DECLARE declaration_statement;
. . .
executable_statement;
RETURN statement;
. . .
END;
```

Note that the RETURNS datatype is mandatory and that there must at least be one RETURN statement.

Using Stored Function

While you use a stored procedure by calling it, you use a stored function in a SQL statement just like you use any built-in function.

Here is an example of calling a stored function named new_price in a SELECT statement. We will create this function a bit later.

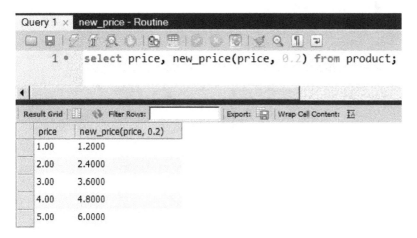

Creating Stored Function in MySQL Workbench

To create a stored function, right-click the Functions under the schema (database) where you want to store the function object; then click the Create Function.

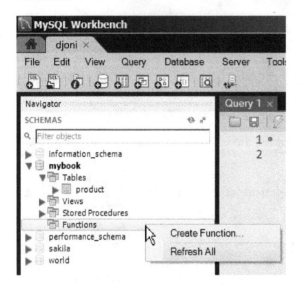

You will be shown a skeleton stored function.

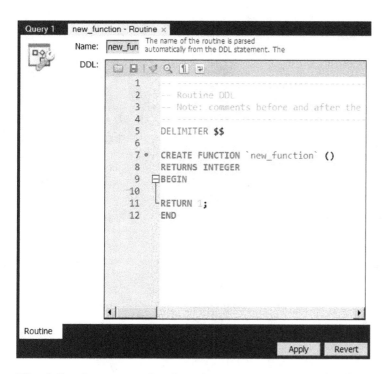

The following new_price function returns a new price for each of the current price. The new_price is the sum of the current price and the increase. The function has two parameters, the current price and increase.

```
CREATE FUNCTION new_price (price DECIMAL(6,2), increase
      DECIMAL(6,2))
RETURNS decimal(8,4)
BEGIN
declare returned_new_price decimal(6,4);
SET returned_new_price = price + (price * increase);
RETURN returned_new_price;
END
```

We can now use the new_price function in a SQL statement, such as for updating the price of our products.

```
UPDATE product
SET price = new_price(price, 0.2);
```

Assuming our product table has the following rows

After executing the update statement, the prices will be as follows.

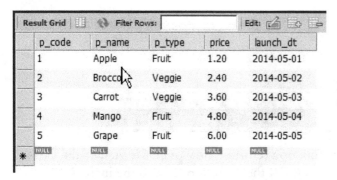

You can update and delete a function similarly to when you update/delete a procedure (see the Update and Delete Procedure topics discussed earlier in Chapter 1)

Appendix A: Installing MySQL Server and Workbench

To try out the examples in this book, you need a MySQL database. Because you need to create tables and other objects, as well as store and update data, it is best if you have your own database. Fortunately, you can download MySQL Community Edition for free from MySQL's website. MySQL is supported on a number of platforms; the following installation guide is for Windows only.

Downloading MySQL Community Edition

This database software can be downloaded from this web page.
http://dev.mysql.com/downloads/mysql/

Scroll down until you see MySQL Installer for Windows on the list. Then, select MySQL Installer MSI by click its Download button. On the next web page, click the "No thanks, just start my download" link, at the bottom left corner. Downloading will start.

Note
The book examples are tested on Windows. They should work equally well on other platforms.

Installing MySQL Community Edition

Execute your downloaded MSI file. Allow the installer to run when you are requested to confirm so, as well when a security warning window appears. . You will see the MySQL Installer Welcome window.

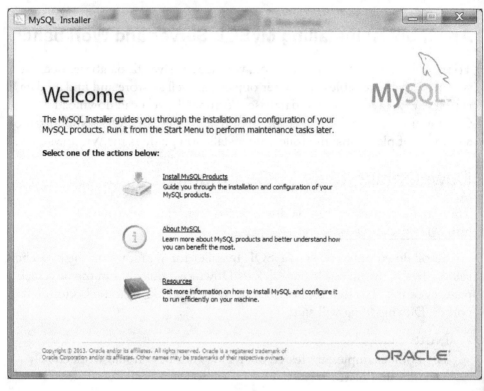

Click the Install MySQL Products, accept the agreement on the License Agreement window, and click the Next button. The next window that will appear is the "Find latest products" window.

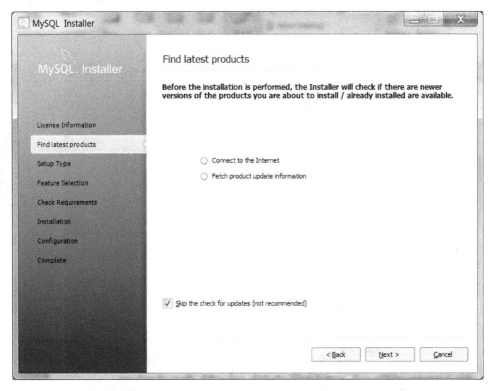

Select the "Skip the check for updates (not recommended)" and click the Next button. The Setup Type window will show up.

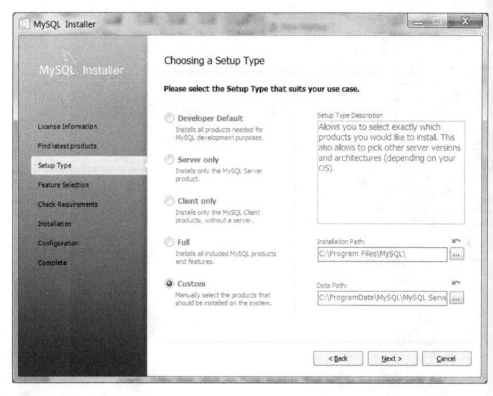

Select Custom, and you will get the Feature Selection window.

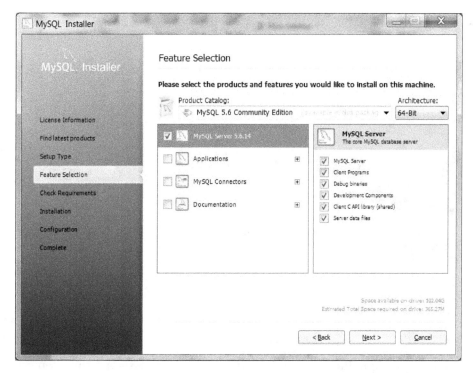

Choose the MySQL Server and Documentation only (the first and last items on the left list) and click Next button. Click Next button again on the next window and then click Execute on the next window. On the next two windows, click Next buttons.

The Configuration window will appear; just click the Next button.

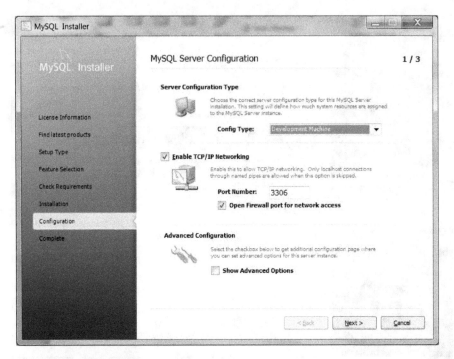

You will be prompted to enter and confirm the root's password, then you can click the Next button.

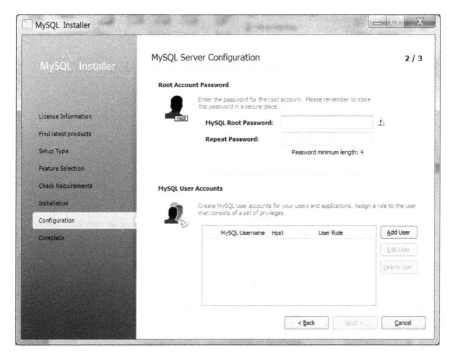

On the next Configuration window, click the Next button. When the installation finishes, click the Finish button.

Your MySQL should have started automatically as a Windows service ready for use.

Installing MySQL Workbench

You can download the Workbench from mysql website. At the time I wrote this book it was available on http://dev.mysql.com/downloads/workbench/

Download the MSI Installer

Execute the mysql-workbench-community-6.1.7-win32.msi downloaded file. You will see a window. Click the Run button.

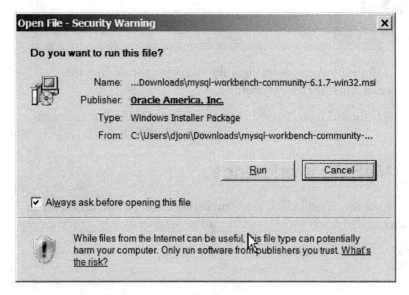

On the Welcome window, click the Next button.

Click the Next button on the next two windows. Then, on the next window click the Install button.

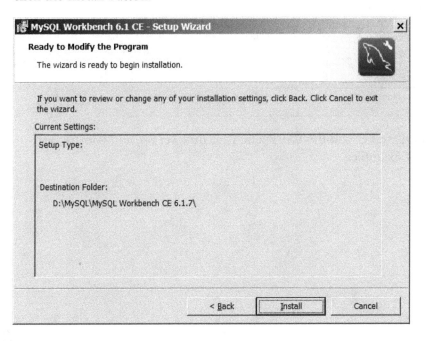

Click the Yes button on the next window. When the completion window shows up, click the Finish button.

You start the Workbench from your Windows Start menu.

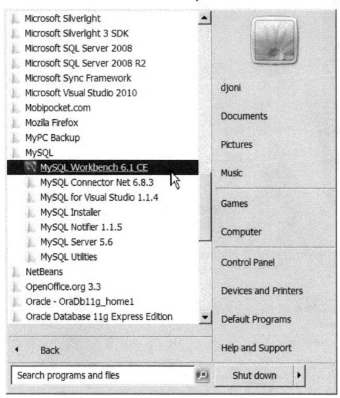

Your MySQL server and the Workbench are now set up, and you are ready to try the book examples.